T0287875

NOMADIC PRESS

OAKLAND

PHILADELPHIA

XALAPA

WWW.NOMADICPRESS.ORG

MASTHEAD
Founding Publisher
J. K. Fowler

ASSOCIATE EDITOR
Michaela Mullin

LEAD EDITOR
Noelia Cerna

DESIGN
Jevohn Tyler Newsome

MISSON STATEMENT Through publications, events, and active community participation, Nomadic Press collectively weaves together platforms for intentionally marginalized voices to take their rightful place within the world of the written and spoken word. Through our limited means, we are simply attempting to help right the centuries' old violence and silencing that should never have occurred in the first place and build alliances and community partnerships with others who share a collective vision for a future far better than today.

INVITATIONS Nomadic Press wholeheartedly accepts invitations to read your work during our open reading period every year. To learn more or to extend an invitation, please visit: www.nomadicpress.org/invitations

DISTRIBUTION
Orders by teachers, libraries, trade bookstores, or wholesalers:

Nomadic Press Distribution
orders@nomadicpress.org
(510) 500-5162

Small Press Distribution
spd@spdbooks.org
(510) 524-1668 / (800) 869-7553

This book was made possible by a loving community of chosen family and friends, old and new.

For author questions or to book a reading at your bookstore, university/school, or alternative establishment, please send an email to info@nomadicpress.org.

Cover art: "These Eyes (The Guess Who)" by Greta Boesel

Published by Nomadic Press, 111 Fairmount Avenue, Oakland, California 94611

First printing, 2022

Library of Congress Cataloging-in-Publication Data

Title: ***In Between Places***
p. cm.

Summary: *In Between Places* lyrically explores family mythology and the fallibility of memory. The poems act as mile markers in a Black woman's literal and figurative journey across decades and across the country, in a search for home in different cities—and people. From a sense of longing and displacement, the collection arrives in a place of stability, resilience, and triumph.

[1. POETRY / Women Authors. 2. POETRY / American / African American & Black. 3. POETRY / Subjects & Themes / Family. 4. POETRY / Subjects & Themes / Places. 5. POETRY / American / General] I. III. Title.

LIBRARY OF CONGRESS CONTROL NUMBER: 2022937158

ISBN: 978-1-955239-30-1

IN BETWEEN PLACES

PLACES

Lauren L. Wheeler

IN BETWEEN PLACES

PLACES

Lauren L. Wheeler

**NOMADIC
PRESS**

*for **PELE**, the best idea I've ever had*

*for **CHARLIE**, the best present I've ever gotten*

*and for **NANA**, whose love kept me alive*

CONTENTS

reading guide

FOREWORD

I remember vividly the first time I experienced the power of Lauren Wheeler's poetry—it was a Sunday afternoon in a lesbian bar in Long Beach, California, where a congregation of fellow misfits squeezed into a tiny space to revel in the gospel of making noise. In a nation where so many of us, as Lauren writes, "cannot afford to be crazy," there are small rooms carved out along the outskirts of every city: intentional universes where historically silenced people gather to either be seen in their most vulnerable forms, or become invisible—participating in a controlled masquerade—that enables their true power to press through to the surface.

Lauren's work straddles both of these worlds with precision and a feral undercurrent. As a colleague who has witnessed the evolution of her writing over the past two decades, I was struck by how evenly keeled this book felt as a whole, and how unrepentant the voice of these poems is when naming a brutal injury while resisting any demands to become a survival anthem. In literature, the journey of Black womanhood is often pinned down by a dangerous expectation to come up with a cure for itself, as if it is some affliction to overcome. *In Between Places* is a gloriously autonomous text, mapping out the rugged landscape of housing uncertainty and parental abandonment, failed relationships and the incessant hammer of anti-Black racism beneath the medicinal atmosphere of chosen kinship and the irrepressible lineage of matriarchal ancestors who are "always leaving from, never going to."

In the poem "Two Ships, Passing," Lauren writes of an elsewhere father:

> "You say, 'I love you,' and now the bartender thinks
> we are on a date. I am tipsy, but I remember who you are.
> 'He's my father,' I say, the words foreign in my mouth.
> This is a tongue I do not speak, a language
> in which I will never be fluent."

At first, a reader might marvel at her unfaltering ability to present so plainly a massive hole in the universe, not as a loss, but as an accepted term of human existence. But the emotional intelligence of Lauren's craft is how efficiently she steers the complicated and awkward energies of absence into a room to be assessed, then released to roam free again. The gift, here, is the glimpse; the intentional withholding that asks us to not just become surveyors of the hole, but to find how we, too, fall into it.

The glory of *In Between Places* is how effortlessly it is a book of praise while avoiding the oft-irresistible forms of sentimentality. Praise the soft architecture of a daughter's hope and the sharpened shadows of her anxiety. Praise the woman in the public bathroom:

> "copper-skinned and statuesque, she stands at the sink
> with one arm raised above her turbaned head, splashes water
> from the tap into an unshaven armpit and mutters to no one
> we can see."

Praise the daughter's envy that covets the gentle hands of her mother, offered to a drunken stranger. Praise the settling into the darkened wings of a stage.

Lauren Wheeler's voice steps into the literary world as a divine and measured disruptor, so sharp and exact, you don't know you've been halved until you've slid down to the floorboards. Here, we are granted permission to name and resurrect our most forgotten selves, to bend our broken bodies into vibrant hallelujahs and submit only to the needs of our liberated and undeniable spirits.

Rachel McKibbens
author of *Pink Elephant,*
Into the Dark and Emptying Field, and *blud*

INTRODUCTION

I'm writing this from the back bedroom of my house in West Oakland, at a standing desk overlooking the backyard with the 980 freeway beyond. I've lived in this house longer than I've lived anywhere else in my life, which began in Chicago and at age ten took me all over the country, sometimes by choice, but oftentimes not. This is a house that I made an offer on, site unseen, from Texas. A house that is big and rambling and 110 years old and breath-taking and in need of many repairs and frustrating and expensive and on Martin Luther King, Jr. Way. And there's just something about that last bit—about there always being a Martin Luther King, Jr. Way or Boulevard or Drive. Always it runs through the Black neighborhood, past proud brownstones or housing projects or well-kept bungalows or despairing Victorians. Always it feels like the cork in the shaken bottle, both reparations for his murder and an easy boundary—a line in the sand.

In the Bay Area, in Oakland, as in many other cities around the country, neighborhoods are being redrawn, boundaries shifting. The irony of my managing to buy this house, on this street. It feels like a reclamation, a reinvestment. I am the first person in my immediate family to own a home since my maternal great-grandparents came to Chicago from Missouri sometime around the turn of the last century. My great-grandfather built his family's house with his own two hands. When it caught fire and burned to the ground, he built it again. I remember visiting cousins in that house when I was a child, its floors slanted, rooms in odd order. But it was still standing, 80 years after he built it. It was the greatest token of love he could give his wife and his 13 children: a home.

When I decided to make an offer on this house, my real estate agent suggested I write the sellers a letter. I dreaded writing it. I didn't want to write something insincere or cloying, but when I finally made myself sit down with paper and pen, what I wrote was anything but insincere. I mentioned that I had considered buying a house in Austin, where I'd moved for work and had been living for two years, but couldn't reconcile it, because Austin wasn't home:

> North Oakland is. West Oakland is. The neighborhoods in which I lived first as a child and then as an adult. The neighborhoods in which I found my dog, Java the Mutt, wandering the streets as a puppy in 2002. (She's 11 now.) The neighborhoods in which I went door to door, getting out the vote, as an electoral volunteer in 2008. The neighborhoods in which my friends and family live as teachers and body workers and community organizers and programmers and bartenders and filmmakers.
> Oakland is home.

It's been nine years since I wrote that letter. Since then, I've had a child, changed jobs, changed partners, changed jobs again, gotten married in the midst of a pandemic, fallen apart, and put myself back together. Java the Mutt died, and two other aging brown pitbull-type creatures, Chai and Nutmeg, provide the canine humor around here. I've spent the last two years in this house with my child and my partner, hiding from COVID and finally nesting, making it feel like mine: filling it with plants, making it more sustainable, cooking meals in it to sustain us and nourish us, continuing to turn it into, as Nato Green wrote about his home, "a house that's all bookshelves." I'm finally home, in a way

I couldn't imagine after so much searching, and it feels like I've given myself and my family the greatest token of love I could.

What does any of that have to do with this book? Everything. How I made it home is what this collection is about. It's not a map, exactly, and definitely not a set of directions. But you could think of it as a travel log, or better yet, postcards from the places and people I've been during the journey.

Thank you for taking this trip with me.

Lauren L. Wheeler
April 2022

"Perhaps home is not a place but simply an irrevocable condition."

James Baldwin, *Giovanni's Room*

COFFEE SHOP, UNION SQUARE IN JUNE

Only the brown busboys with Spanish mouths
wear shirts proclaiming them staff. The hipless waitresses'
other job is a runway, so they practice "aloof" when walking me
through the air-conditioned front room to a table in the back
where the AC's broken. They bring me a $17 domestic beer.
I am paying for ambiance and perspiration.

I read four of my new sister's poems and go outside for a cigarette.
Voices and traffic are muted by subterranean city hum.
Other buildings hoard cold air as my forehead grows slick.

Back inside, I walk through the front room grateful
for a brief reprieve from the sidewalk's steam and take my seat.
"One more?" my server asks.
"One more."

LADY LIBERTY

"Give me your tired, your poor,
Your huddled masses yearning to breathe free,
The wretched refuse of your teeming shore.
Send these, the homeless, tempest-tost to me,
I lift my lamp beside the golden door!"

Emma Lazarus, "The New Colossus"

As the sky swings its fiery fist towards noon, I retreat
from the diminishing shade of Bryant Park to the cool interior
of the New York Public Library: clutching two slim volumes of poetry,
I wind my way through high-ceilinged halls, trustees' names etched
into their walls with gold leaf, looking for a place to read.

Ducking groups of gawking tourists with Midwestern complexions
and cameras hanging from their necks, I resist taking my own pictures,
remember the admonishment against flash photography at the entrance.
In the air-conditioned digital gallery, I find a chair but continue
to wonder where they keep the books.

I head to the toilets downstairs where tourists wait awkwardly
outside the women's restroom, and I smell their discomfort before
I see her: copper-skinned and statuesque, she stands at the sink
with one arm raised above her turbaned head, splashes water from the tap
into an unshaven armpit and mutters to no one we can see.

I press past her, my bladder unconcerned; here, in this washroom,
are all human stink. When I emerge from the stall, she is gone,
the floor shining wet from her morning ablutions: a respite
from the city's grim patina within these hallowed halls
where we all, each of us, can feel at home.

IN BETWEEN PLACES

Brownstone, Mediterranean, hi-rise, Victorian, Craftsman, clapboard houses, 60s stucco slums, basement apartments.

Late, and then Past Due, and then Final Notice, and then Duraflame logs in the fireplace for heat and homework done by kerosene lamp.

Moving boxes, masking tape, Sharpies, moving vans, pickup trucks and station wagons, self-storage units.

Eviction notices, piles of garbage, toys left behind: white stuffed dog, two years' worth of Lego blocks, pink and purple roller skates with glittery butterflies on the heel. Boxes of books, camping equipment, a sewing machine never seen again. Two puppies tied briefly to a parking meter (crying brought them back) then later abandoned for good at the pound (crying brought a smack).

Rooms, and couches, and fold-outs, and cots, and floors. Lots of floors. Cars, two motels, a friend's mother's double-wide, the shelter that one time.

Airports and train stations and subways and freeways and bus stops and parks.

Always leaving from, never going to.

SALVATION

When what passes for parents can't get a divorce
because they can't get married, they split
the only way they know how: loud as sirens.
The color red figures prominently. My mother's girlfriend
is a terrible person, but her paycheck helped pay the rent.
Tonight we'll sleep on a couch in a stranger's apartment.
We've been summoned here as angels of mercy.
The stranger is passed out on the floor,
her jeans around her thighs, piss pooling beneath her drunken body.
My mother touches her with gentle hands I envy.
Drags her into the bathtub, voice soft as she wipes away vomit
and urges a washcloth between the woman's legs.
Later, once my mother has dressed her in a nightgown
and put her to bed, I notice how pretty she is.
Tomorrow, I will learn her name, and she and my mother
will be friends for the short remainder of her life.
But tonight, names are unimportant.
We are all *Life Jacket* or *Oxygen Mask*.
Desperate, perhaps, to be something else:
tonight we are *Solace* and *Safety*.
Tonight we are saved.

AN AX AT THE DOOR

One morning when I was 11, I walked into the living room just as an ax came through the front door. It was the fire department. My mother had swallowed a handful of pain pills and called 911 just before she passed out.

This is one of those things that happened when I was young that I forget about and then, when I remember, forget is not normal. I don't know what normal is, but I assume it's not waking up to your mother's suicide attempts.

Maybe that morning is not indelibly marked on me because it wasn't the first time my mother had tried to abandon me. When I was a baby, she moved to San Diego and tried to kill herself. Then she came back to Chicago, but she left again. She always left again.

Having forgotten about this thing that happened when I was young, I thought of it last night, talking to my lover about my most recent attempt to get my mother to see a therapist. My mother is a therapist, but she refuses to see one.

I nudge, cajole, bully, beg. After years of antidepressants and anti-anxiety meds and anti- everything, she's a moving shadow. She ignores me, goes to the White Horse, drinks too much tequila, dates rough women who beat her and put her in the hospital, won't call the ones with jobs and no substance abuse issues.

My 20 psych visits at the sliding-scale clinic are coming to a close. My therapist likes me, thinks I'd make a good therapist. I flinch when she says it, but now I'm researching grad schools, ordering transcripts, writing essays, begging for letters of recommendation.

I'd like to ask my therapist for a letter of recommendation. I'd like to ask my therapist for a clean bill of health. I'd like to ask her for a warranty, a guarantee, a promise that I won't be a moving shadow, that I won't abandon my children, that they'll never see an ax coming through the living room door.

FAMILY HISTORY

A hundred people watch open-mouthed
as two women run through Roseland, chasing
my grandmother Rena's first husband with an ice pick.
My great-aunt Alene and her best friend Julia Browning
will eventually become mothers of the church.

Because God helps those who help themselves.

SUNDOWNING

She's tired.
That's the first thing she says
when my mother and I arrive
and she's lying
in a hospital bed hooked up
to the dialysis machine.
Her hands, gnarled from years
of cleaning and cooking,
hands that held me when I was small,
smaller than she is now, eyes closed,
reaching out for something invisible.

That's the only thing lucid
she says in the time we sit with her,
after they've brought her back
to her own bed in her own room,
after three hours on the machine that works
for kidneys too tired to clean
her blood anymore.

She asks if Harry is still out there in the hall—
Harry, her younger brother who lives
in Chicago. She won't eat her food, claims she's
had dinner already, but that's not true.

She's upset by the number of times
they take her temperature, won't stop
talking, complaining, the thin plastic
thermometer bobbing under her tongue.
She's convinced the pills they give her
are giving her these crazy dreams,
making her mind go too fast.

My mother asks the nurse what they are.
"Tylenol." "Tylenol with codeine?"
"No, just Tylenol."
Tylenol, and vitamins, and other pills
to bring down her blood pressure,
which is still too high. "But it's lower now,"
she says. "I don't want any more pills."

She wants to go home. Blindly dials numbers
on the hospital phone that doesn't call out.
"Who are you calling?" my mother asks,
and she snaps at her—"I'm 96 years old.
I don't ask you who you call."
She says she's calling Bill, her cousin,
dead for decades. He'll come and get her.
He'll take her home.

"I'm tired," she says,
mouths more words to people
who aren't there and falls asleep.

TWO SHIPS, PASSING

"Ships that pass in the night and speak each other in passing;
Only a signal shown and a distant voice in the darkness;
So on the ocean of life we pass and speak one another,
Only a look and a voice; then darkness again and a silence."

Henry Wadsworth Longfellow, "The Theologian's Tale"

1. The first time you see me is proof
    there's no such thing as love
    at first sight: me, a few hours old,
    in an incubator in a Chicago hospital.
    Peering into the nursery, you pick
    the wrong baby. My mother
    corrects you, points me out.
    You say, "But she looks white."

2. I am 19 when you walk past me at Penn Station
    an hour after you were supposed to meet me,
    you in a beat-up motorcycle jacket and Bauhaus t-shirt,
    me with a shaved head and a nose ring
    that briefly convince you I am my mother
    playing a cruel trick. We ride
    the packed PATH train together in silence.

When we arrive at your house in Jersey City,
I'm out of cigarettes: an opportunity for you to escape
an awkward reunion and give me something I need.

Later that night, your wife Zoe suggests another remedy
after my brother is tucked away in bed. Do I smoke reefer, she asks,
and orders you to retrieve the weed from your room upstairs.
"You're not going to hide it from her," she says.
"It's too late to start being a father now."

3.   We decide to meet at a BBQ joint on the Lower East Side.
     It is years later, I'm living in California now, and this time,
     it is just us—no stepmother, no half-brother. Just us.
     Too nervous to eat, we sit at the bar, drink Manhattans.
     You are funny, and I hear your laughter in mine.
     As the bourbon flows, we become easy with each other.
     You promise to help me if I go to grad school;
     you apologize for your decades of absence.

     You say, "I love you," and now the bartender thinks
     we are on a date. I am tipsy, but I remember who you are.
     "He's my father," I say, the words foreign in my mouth.
     This is a tongue I do not speak, a language
     in which I will never be fluent.

     I never see you again.

CHICAGO

I grew up in the cracks
between my parents like
a weed, stubborn evidence
of what happens when
fertile soil goes untended.

DON'T TAKE RIDES FROM STRANGERS

but what if class starts in 20 minutes and the bus is running late and the stranger is white, in his late twenties or early thirties, slender build, average height (maybe a little on the short side—it's hard to tell from my impatient perch on the your-ad-here bench). And he's dressed in a fine green single-breasted suit and has nice hair and a neatly-trimmed goatee. And he's wearing expensive sunglasses, somewhat superfluous since clouds are obscuring the descending sun, and he definitely won't need them by the time he reaches his destination, which, he says, is Beverly Hills.

And I'll bet he smells good, too, designer cologne enveloping the leather interior of his shiny new European SUV. I imagine some fragrance so sophisticated I haven't even heard of it choking me in the passenger seat as he bites my neck, one hand tangled in my hair, the other yanking at my pants, even though his knee, pressed between my thighs, is making it difficult for him to pull them off. In some remote and vacant parking lot, power locks prevent me from escaping what has become a cell on wheels, and my screams are muffled by German engineering. As he fumbles his way inside, he groans and hisses against my ear, "You know, you should never take rides from strangers."

Class starts in 7 minutes and the bus has just now come and as I board, I'm still staring east down Santa Monica Boulevard, wondering if I would have made it on time.

DOLORES PARK

spring-loaded, she flips onto her back,
brown eyes giggling in the silly dog-head,
tongue hanging out, her clumsy feet in the air,
as the mastiff sniffs her, paws her chest,
and dashes away, laughing.

VALENCIA STREET ON A SUMMER NIGHT

The howling of boozehounds
outside the bar across the street
blends with the ear-splitting yodel
of police cars and fire trucks speeding
to the latest Mission catastrophe.

I would close the windows,
but it's hot in here. The air should be Republican,
it's so oppressive. In the kitchen,
the fan squeaks near the ceiling, useless and
archaic as a butter churn, rotary phone, Victrola.

It's so hot and only getting hotter.
By the time the mosquitoes arrive,
all whirring cellophane wings,
I'm just a pile of sounds beside you,
moans and purrs and cries wrapped in skin.

The night sighs as red digits switch places,
ushering in the morning's music:
garbage trucks, the alarm's faint bleating,
and, occasionally, the chirp of a lone bird.

SLEEP CORRUPTS HER

The mascara
she was too tired to remove
migrated to her cheeks during the night,
crusted in the corners of her eyes.
Her skin gleams feverish and tight,
etched with lines the pillow made,
like sand after high tide.

Once ruby lips now resemble
bruised plums and, parted
slightly as she snores, reveal
the stink of whiskey and decay.

Good morning. She yawns, blinks.
Good morning. He smiles a few inches away,
thinks: *She's never looked*
more beautiful than she does right now.

THE GREATEST SHOW ON EARTH

1. UNDER THE BIG TOP

Your bed smells faintly
of sweat and sawdust and maybe
elephants, but I can't say for sure.
Lying beside you I blink
when I see a bear on a unicycle
ride past your window.

It's probably a bike messenger, you say,
and go back to sleep. I want to believe you,
like I believed the man in satin pantaloons
flying by last night hadn't been shot
out of a cannon. It's a carrier pigeon, you said.

I rub my eyes and know my makeup is smeared and wonder
what I look like to you: a trapeze princess
with teeth like piano keys? Then I remember
you saying everyone loves a clown.

The one juggling chainsaws outside the restaurant
almost ruined our first date, but when you kissed me,
I savored the taste of peanuts on your tongue,
forgot the high wire we were standing on,
ignored the lack of a net below.

2. SIDESHOW

For a nickel, you can take a picture of me
standing just so in front of a wooden board
with a heart painted on it.

For a dime, you can take a picture with me,
you squatting behind and peeking through
like I'm one of those cardboard cutouts
of an "Indian Chief" or a unicorn or some other
supposedly mythical creature.

When you offer a quarter, we move to the tent,
dim-lit and dusty, where I sit on the low
quilt-covered cot and pat the space beside me.
You are nervous. "Will it hurt?"

I shake my head. "It never hurts. Not anymore."
Then I take your hand and guide it up towards
the hole in my chest. You tremble for a second
as you reach through me, wiggle your fingers
around behind my back, disbelieving.

"Where is your heart?" you ask.
"How do you live without your heart?"
I take your hand again, kiss it.
"It's amazing the things you can learn
to live without."

THIS MISSION

The Indian ice cream shop is gone,
my old brunch spot is a hookah bar now,
the combination pet supply store/hair salon
next door to my old apartment building
has brown paper at its windows. The lefty
bookstore and crêperie will be next.
Gentrification is the only permanent fixture here.

Friendships splinter into uncomfortable civility
and then nothing at all. Lovers slam doors
and become ex-lovers. We move a few blocks down,
move to the East Bay, or give up entirely and
change states, go somewhere new
without all the reminders of what used to be here,
what used to be important,
what's missing.

THROUGH THE PEEPHOLE

When I spy you through the peephole after you knock on my door, I open it and say, "So, what are you doing?" and you say, looking down, not looking me in the eye, "Ruining my life," and walk in. We sit in my living room, you perched on the edge of the old futon, hands folded on your knees. I ask you if you want a drink, and you say yes. You sip at the whiskey and coke, take a drag from the pipe I pass you, and talk. You don't tell me why you've come here to ruin your life, and I'm listening intently for what you're not saying. I want to hear the reason you've decided to make an apocalypse out of me. I notice you don't talk about him, don't say his name. I stand up and move towards you, hold the pipe against your lips until you pull back, smoke tumbling out of you like my own tiny dragon. I pull you to your feet and kiss your closed mouth, your cheek, the side of your neck. You murmur something into my hair, and I wait. Maybe you've changed your mind. Maybe you're going to walk back out that door, go home to him, save yourself. I listen. "Please," you whisper against my ear. I walk you backwards towards the bedroom, backwards to the end of your life.

ALIBI GIRL

I'm the alibi girl—a convenient excuse when you need one.
I'll write you a hall pass, always let you pass go.
I'll be your get-out-of-jail-free card
despite all my convictions.

There's a price that gets paid for such generosity,
and I usually pick up the check, leave a big tip, and spend
nights in the fetal position alone, wondering when I'll be
more than an easy way out, more than just easy.

What happens if the alibi goes missing,
a fugitive from charges of aiding and abetting?
Alibis are lies made flesh,
and sometimes the flesh is weak.
So cut out my tongue. I'll nod my head when you want me to
but spare myself the sound of my voice,
the sound of promises I've made, breaking.

TEXAS

Austin in the summer
is the guy with really bad breath
who stands too close at parties
and won't shut up.

MUSCLE MEMORY

There's always an explanation:
        Step-by-step instructions.
        Quick reference guide.
        A handbook.

How to   fall in love.
How to   fall out of it.

(Amazing that with all the falling around here, no one gets hurt.)

Step 1: Smile.
Step 2: Get used to smiling.

We'll get to Step 3 in a minute.
First, a caveat: Someone always gets hurt.

Read the disclaimer. It's hidden
        in every package
        under the wrapper
        in really small print.

Muscles remember.
        The heart is a muscle.

Break it,
it may forgive you.
But it'll never forget.

Blame it on muscle memory.
History is etched into every fiber,
myelin's alive with stories.
Their telling is a reflex.

A heartbeat
        an involuntary movement,
        a repetitive motion.

Heartbeat,
        a repetitive motion.
Heartbeat,
        repetitive stress.
Injuries, revisited.

History is etched into every fiber,
every fiber is doomed to repeat it.
"We will never forget," they chant.
We will never forget.

NOTE: It takes 43 muscles to frown and 17 to smile.

Step 3: Keep smiling.

The heart gets stuck in an endless loop,

a broken record,
a record skipping—

A record is evidence.
Proof that you were there.

If a tree falls in the forest,
and no one's there to hear it
          just record it.

Step 4: Go back to Step 3.
It's that damn muscle memory again.

Play it back.
          Side A: The first time your heart was broken.
          Side B: The first time your heart was broken.
It'll never forget.

History is etched into its fibers,
myelin's alive with stories.
Their telling is a reflex
          the heart a record skipping.

Step 5: Go back to Step 1.
Your muscles will remember.

HYBRID VIGOR

We look at each other, wait for internal dialogue
to die down. In silence, hobbled tongues reach
towards each other. Bodies talk when mouths can't
find words: a secret handshake, semaphore, Morse
code-switching, languages cobbled together:
pidgin, creole, Spanglish, "bad" English, ebony phonics,
survival tactics made beautiful, polished to copper shine.
Pennies are most valuable to those who haven't got a dime.

TREADING WATER

1. If only days were a little
   shorter, I'd feel like a success
   at something—the short trip
   to the bathroom in the morning,
   a dog walked around the block,
   perhaps even a small meal prepared
   by my own hands or at least eaten,
   regardless of the cook.
   But days are run-on sentences
   of failure, served consecutively.
   Hours taste like mercury
   from a broken thermometer,
   bitter and insoluble in my mouth.

2. Hope is not as strong as rope
   swinging from a chandelier.
   It breaks, disintegrates
   into threads of confusion

(did I call this love?)and mistaken identity
(did I love you?)
but still I tie it snug
around my neck, bear scars
from a noose of optimism.

3. My heart doesn't go
    on vacation nearly enough.
    If it did, it could handle
    the suffocating silence, swagger
    of invincibility, collect calls
    from the abyss you've plunged into,
    slurred defenses that all sound
    like "save me" even as
    you kick me underwater
    trying to save yourself.

4. Your days are also too long.
    I wish I could shorten them,
    trim away the split-ends of disaster,
    defuse your ticking bomb. Instead
    I get ungrateful shrapnel, metallic
    reminders of my own failings
    mixed with the added scattershot of yours.

5. My eyes scan the horizon for a lifeboat,
    but all I see is the sun putting off setting,
    drawing out dusk like the last breath
    you take before making a decision.
    I tie my new scarf around you,
    throw the end towards the shore, and pray
    it catches.

STANDING OVATION

You grip the microphone
like it will save your life.
In front of an audience dim
past the stage lights, you shine.

I've been waiting in the wings,
more open than the 500 strangers
who throw your fliers in the trash
as soon as you finish your set.

Hours after you've broken
their hearts in the spotlight,
you break mine:
in the dark, in your bed,
you turn away from the universe
I offer you: pockmarked with stars,
the scars of comets crashing,
you are violently beautiful.
I have traveled light-years to touch
this skin you hate living in.

Beyond the darkened crowd,
beneath the applause of a room
full of strangers, is my heart: the one
that beats for you like the whole world
begging for an encore.

BODY ROCK, OCTOBER 8TH

When the DJ transitions
from old-school hip hop, R&B,
and world beat to straight-up
merengue, I am able to put things
into perspective and sum up
the fundamental problems
in our relationship thusly:
I'm tired of always being the one to lead.

THE BED

This bed was an upgrade from the last,
frame bought online and stored
in an ex's garage for months, the mattress
the cheapest I could afford that wasn't
on Craigslist. It was a double,
and we took up too much space,
especially with the dog always
between us sprawled sideways, yelping
and kicking in her sleep, some make-believe
squirrel just out of reach.

The new bed is sturdy despite the Allen wrench
assembly. A platform base with drawers for linens,
no squeaking or rattling, though also
no convenient place to hang the flogger
a different ex gave me for my birthday
years ago. This mattress is similar to one
I slept on at an upscale hotel, and it's a queen.
There's plenty of space for both—
for all three—of us.

This bed feels abandoned even when we're in it.
In this bed, we only sleep and not even well,
tossing and turning, twisting the sheets
out of discomfort instead of passion. I grip
a pillow between my thighs
and dream of you. When I wake,
you're on the other side, your back to me.

I remember when my bed was for more
than nursing insomnia: alternating between
love and sleep for hours, hands slipping
up and over and beneath and between:
a pile of prepositions, bodies
the fulfillment of so many
propositions, skin touching skin
as promise, hair a damp tangle
as we stared at each other,
inches apart.

There are compromises we all make
for love: I'm no walk in the park,
and I know that: I'm moody, I'm messy,
and I drink too much, work too much,
complain too much. I am a professional
complainer; I should have business cards made.

I found my first white pubic hair
three days after I turned 35. My pussy
has officially raised the white flag. I do not recall
the last time we had sex and it did not feel
like a chore neither of us wanted to do.
I do not recall the last time we had sex, full stop.
I do not recall the last time I slept next to you
and felt like more than a security
blank with a heartbeat.

The new bed did not fix anything.
Talking did not fix anything.
Yelling did not fix anything.
Couples counseling did not fix anything.
The flogger, the books on the nightstand,
the box of toys did not fix anything.
My love—my love—

I am learning that sometimes, when things are broken,
I cannot will them to mend. I cannot wish away
fractures. I cannot pretend the fracture is not there,
cutting jagged between our sleepless bodies a chasm
we can never cross. A new bed is just a new stage

for old drama: a play I did not write, a tragedy
in which I did not ask to be cast. Now I close my eyes,
force myself into uneasy sleep where I wander
into another production that ends so differently,
where there's romance and laughter
and maybe a baby crying between its parents instead
of a ten-year-old stray. But I wake up blinking,
wiping sand from my eyes, trying to
hold onto the dream.

AT THE SLAM

While counting the money at the door,
Joyce tucks wads of cash
into her bra, and I'm awed
into hilarious simile
and excessive colon usage:
breasts like bank vaults:
locked down, impenetrable,
and full of so much promise:
or, what you imagine the best day
of your life might feel like.

WHY SHE ALWAYS WORE PANTS AFTER HER DIVORCE

Mourning black
would have been
too obvious, so she
just stopped shaving
anything
      below
          the
              waist.

THE DRESS

for Tara Betts, with apologies to
Ernest Hemingway but not really

FOR SALE: WEDDING DRESS, NEVER WORN.

I've done this before. Years ago, in a late-night, unemployed mania,
I decided to purge my belongings: boxes of sentiment
shuttled from apartment to apartment, lover to lover:
poems written for me on bar napkins and then tucked, forgotten,
between the pages of old notebooks yellow with a decade's regret.

I considered Ebay. That one always wanted to be famous,
and what is fame if not strangers bidding on your broken promises?
But the landfill called his name the loudest. I surrendered
those fragments to a mountain of over, of finished, of done.

Now, moving from our uncareful cocoon of the last year, I toss
armfuls of clothing into the beat-up luggage my grandmother left me.
My grandmother left me leaving. She also left me pragmatism:
"Wish in one hand, spit in the other, and see which fills the fastest.

As I heave my past into trash bags and suitcases, shaking hands clutch
a white dress cloaked in plastic. Two summers ago,

As I heave my past into trash bags and suitcases, shaking hands clutch
a white dress cloaked in plastic. Two summers ago, I chased this gown
like a fawn through Manhattan department stores. Now I fold it gently
into a suitcase, nestle a ring box beside it—
another gilded, empty trophy—
and hope it won't take another decade to let them go.

HOW TO BE SINGLE

Sage is purifying. Get a smudge stick.
If you can't find one, your sister-friend
will send it to you from your home coast.
Carry it burning into every room.

Take up weed again. Smoking doesn't make
everything better, but it makes
everything bearable, and on some days,
things will be unbearable: the quiver of loss,
an earthquake in your chest, will drive you
almost mad. You cannot afford to be crazy.
Pack a bowl, light it, breathe in.

Find someone to uncage your body: peel back skin
and make your skeleton dance, a marionette of bones.
Choose someone for whom you will not hate
yourself later, but do not allow yourself to want
too much. For now, you are not looking
for a heart transplant but a crash cart.

Clear.

Cut off your hair. It will scare away
unsuitable callers, and you will stun yourself
in the mirror in the morning, beauty
you believed extinguished shocking
out of your still unsettled pores.

Do not give in to the maw of loneliness.
Over time, it will dull, recede. Force yourself
to tolerate silence, the empty bed, the sound
of your own breathing as you hover near sleep.
Eventually, you will remember that you like solitude.
Eventually, you will remember
that you like yourself.

DOG SITTING

Three days into dog sitting for a friend,
Java the Mutt is no longer scratching at window sills and
destroying door jambs. She is strangely calm,

happy to go for walks through the neighborhood
side by side with a smaller brown dog that looks so much
like her, people assume they're related. She is excited
to wrestle on my bed while I'm still in it. She is content
to lie peacefully beside the crated dog when I am at work
even though she has gnawed through ten crates
in her ten years of living with me.

I come home after a couple of vodka cocktails
and painting with watercolors at a neighbor's apartment.
When the three of us climb into bed, the other dog
curls up near my feet with his favorite bone.

Java sits upright near my head, staring at me
in the darkness. She needs to tell me something.
"I'm lonely," she says. "I know," I say. "So am I."
I put an arm around her warm, furry body,
and we sleep.

NOTHING PERSONAL

Desperately seeking absolutely nothing.
Race and religion unimportant,
gender inconsequential,
species doesn't matter that much.
I'm not interested in your interests,
what books you've read,
whether or not you like animals
or cuddling or bondage.
Moonlit strolls on the beach and
cozy nights by the fire don't do it for me.
While I do like a good bottle of wine,
I want it in a brown paper bag.
The only romantic comedies I want to watch
are snuff films; you're the star.
I'm not looking to be saved,
just a safe word and a razor blade or two.
And no, I don't want an "LTR"—
I don't even need to know your name.
You'd better be gone by the time
my alarm goes off: I'm timing you.

MOMENTUM

1. When asked to describe what you look like, I say,
"waiting." There is no other word for the uneasy lean.
Even when still, your fingers drum, your knee bounces.
There is a whole life one breath away from you, and yet,
you wait.

2. Time is a mass hallucination. The sun comes up,
the sun goes down. We mark calendars, but what tells me
that today is not yesterday? That today is not tomorrow?
I know that time has passed and that nothing has changed
because there is evidence that a bird rested on your left
shoulder. Leaves stained orange with autumn congregate
near your ankles. A spider has found your stagnation
perfectly inviting: webs connect your nose to your chest,
a tiny highway of glass.

3. This morning, I woke when the sun came up, and all day,
in every gesture, a smile: pouring coffee, reading
a magazine before work, writing this poem. Time is not
my enemy. Time is passing, yes, and today, I am smiling.
I am smiling at the sun, and the sun is smiling back.
Time is passing, and I am moving: together, a sundial.
Tomorrow, we will do it again.

THAT WAY

I know you didn't mean it that way, but today is a day
when you're the fifth person who didn't mean it, and the other two
meant it very well, and I just can't keep my mouth shut anymore

because I said nothing when white hipster boys biking in the Mission,
muttering "nigger" *ironically* as they passed. I said nothing
but wished them witness to a small cabin in Missouri

with tiny dark windows like missing teeth, miles from anything
resembling a main road, clothes waving lazily from the line stretched
across the yard and illuminated by the cross being set on fire,

inside babies smacked by helpless women trying to keep them quiet
while outside horses whinny and sigh and bullets and rope are eased
from saddlebags, the night so disgraced that even the moon flinches.

No, I cannot keep my mouth shut any longer, I'm sorry. So when
your eyes grow wide and indignant at being found out, when your face twists
into tantrum, your cheeks streaked with fat embarrassed tears,

I find myself trapped between compassion and a desire
for you to grow a thicker skin: a darker skin, perhaps, for Lord knows
the rest of us can't afford to be so sensitive, so tender,
in this world full of people who never mean it that way.

BULL'S EYES

Standing on a BART train surrounded by children who look like children I might have some day, little boys with their heads shaved close, little girls with hair in braids, tiny plastic barrettes in the shape of birds and fish and flowers clamped at the ends. I'm refreshing my smartphone as I travel back to Oakland early on this BART train under the bay, looking to see what our lives are worth to those twelve people sitting on that jury at the other end of the state, where other juries have decided in the past that our lives are, simply, not worth very much.

But my smartphone isn't so smart under the bay, and instead I smile at the children surrounding me who are acting like children: climbing over their seats, climbing over each other, voices raised in the sparkling cacophony that happy children are known for. They are on their way home from a long day of field-tripping with young white teachers who look exhausted and protective when a middle-aged white man in a suit presses past the children with his briefcase clutched to his chest and his face a mask of annoyance. I wonder if he sees these children as children, or if he sees these children as so many animals, or a drain on the system, or a shitty way to end his workday, or living, breathing bull's eyes. What do the other people around me see when they look at these little boys, smelling like little boys, full of energy and excitement, their eyes reflecting nothing but the sun as we come above ground in West Oakland?

I refresh my phone again and know what our lives are worth, know that the twelve people on that jury decided that these children are little bull's eyes. I want to hold them all close to me, spread my arms around them, protect them from those who will involuntarily pull out their guns, take aim, and slaughter them for being little boys, for being little boys full of energy, for being children who look like children I might have some day.

TETHER

My son's umbilical cord
was tied in a *true knot*
and wrapped around his neck
four times. There's no greater evidence
that historical trauma is genetic
than your child trying to lynch himself
in your womb.

GHOST TOWN

There's a freeway behind my house,
hovering over its shoulder
like a falling knife.

I cannot tell if it is safer for my son to play
in the backyard, where the soil is pregnant with lead,
or out front, which is also pregnant with lead:
there's a slug still stuck in the front gate from
a shooting Thanksgiving weekend, 2009.
My gray hatchback took a bullet in the bumper
my first fall here, four years later.

This street used to be called Grove Street.
Now it's called Martin Luther King Junior Way.
In Chicago, where I was born, I lived on
Martin Luther King Junior Drive.
Hundreds of streets all over the country named
for a victim of America, a consolation prize.

It's not even a good freeway. It's a connector:
it connects one shitty freeway with another shitty freeway.
It's not a freeway one would write songs about, or poems,
though I could tell you a story about the night a cougar
crept across it into the plum and oak trees at the rear of my yard
and terrorized a family of raccoons. My neighbor and I
whispered to each other across the fence in the dark,
hands clutching makeshift weapons, listening to chittering

and then a low, deep-throated growl and then a thump
before the cat's pale silhouette eased down a tree trunk
and skulked back towards the cars speeding
to downtown Oakland and points further south.

The freeway is a dividing line, previously a redline.
The reason no one fixed the pot holes until
three years after I moved here, a middle-class Black
harbinger of gentrification.

The freeway is a dividing line (maybe still a redline),
but I saw a white woman with fuschia hair jog past earlier today,
unbothered by the falling knife or the lead or the mountain lion
or the dead Black man this road is named after,
or the one shot at the corner last week,
so property values must be going up.

READING GUIDE

FAMILY MYTHOLOGY

Write a fairy tale based on a story about your family.

- Who is the hero of the story? Who is the villain?
- Regardless of how the "real" story ended, does your fairy tale have a happy ending?

Create a biography for a family member you never met.

- What did they look like? Do you look like them?
- Imagine what they sounded like and how they spoke. Did they have an accent? Was their voice raspy or high-pitched? What was a phrase they were known for?
- What message would they have wanted to pass on to you?

Write a poem from the perspective of one of your descendants about you as their ancestor.

- What would you be known for? How would they remember you?
- What would be engraved on your tombstone?
- How did you die?

Related poems: *Family History; Salvation; Sundowning; An Ax at the Door; Chicago; Two Ships, Passing*

HERE AND THERE

Write about somewhere you've lived — a country, a city, a house, an apartment.

- When you consider it, which senses are most awakened in your memories? Do you strongly recall how the place smelled, or do you think about it being brightly lit? Does a specific color come to mind?
- If that place were a person, would they be a friend, an enemy, or a lover?
- What would the place say about your time there?

Write about the perfect city.

- What do the buildings look like? What are they made of?
- Who would live there? How would the people there treat each other? How would your city's society function?

Write about life as a nomad.

- What does being a nomad mean to you?
- What are the benefits? What are the costs?
- If you were a nomad, what are the things you would always carry with you?

Related poems: *Coffee Shop, Union Square in June; Lady Liberty; In Between Places; Texas; Valencia Street on a Summer Night; This Mission; Dolores Park; Ghost Town*

STAR-CROSSED

Create a story about a stranger you've seen in public.

- What's their name? Who's their family?
- Imagine the kind of day they are having. What happened to them before you encountered them? What happens to them later on?

Write a letter to an ex-lover or a former friend.

- What did you learn about yourself from your relationship with them? What do you hope they learned from you?
- What would you most want to tell them that you've never been able to say?
- What do you wish for them in the future? Do you wish them well? Do you wish them ill?
- If you wish them ill, what kind of hex would you put on them?

Write an apology to someone.

- What did you do?
- What impact did it have on the other person?
- What will you do differently in the future?

Related poems: *Lady Liberty; Salvation; Two Ships, Passing; Alibi Girl; Through the Peephole; Treading Water; Body Rock, October 8th; The Bed; That Way; Bull's Eyes*

ACKNOWLEDGMENTS

First of all, I would like to acknowledge that many of the poems in this book were written on the unceded territory of Huichin, ancestral home of the Chochenyo-speaking Ohlone people.

Thank you to the publications that gave a home to earlier versions of some of these poems:

"Sleep Corrupts Her" and "Alibi Girl" appeared in *PANK Magazine* online, April 2009.

"Alibi Girl" and the first section of "The Greatest Show on Earth" ("Under the Big Top") were published in *PANK #4*, January 2010.

The second section of "The Greatest Show on Earth" ("Sideshow") was published in *The Nervous Breakdown* in December 2012.

"Why She Always Wore Pants After the Divorce" appeared in *Monkeybicycle* in February 2013.

Thank you to the teachers and professors who saw me and encouraged me to keep writing: Beverly Muskat, Ellen Kempler, Ken McClane, and Archie Ammons.

Thank you to the poetry slam and spoken word scenes that offered a home for my early work and voice and offered me community across the country — San Francisco, Berkeley, Ithaca, New York, Chicago, Los Angeles, Austin, and Oakland.

Thank you to ForWord Girls, Writers With Drinks, the Queer Open Mic, S.F. Literation Front, The New Sh!t Show, Pink Door Writing Retreat, Black Nerd Problems, and the Interdisciplinary Writers Lab for space, for a stage, for your commitment to the craft and collaboration, for feedback, for friendship, for opening my ears, my eyes, my heart.

Thank you to Greta Boesel for allowing me to adorn this book in the magic of her art.

Thank you to J. K. Fowler at Nomadic Press, who made the decision at the beginning of the pandemic to gestate this collection; to Michaela Mullin, for her boundless patience and bringing it to term; and to Noelia Cerna, for her keen insights, body-doubling, support, and outright fiendish cackling that helped me push this one out.

Finally, I would like to send my endless gratitude to the people, across the country and here in the Bay, who have held me through joy and triumph, devastation and loss; who have listened; who have read; who have sat silently; who have cheered; who have made this life not just bearable but one in which I can thrive. You are my family, and without you, I would not be here. And if you're not sure if I'm talking about you, I am.

Lauren L. Wheeler

Lauren L. Wheeler writes poetry, fiction, and about the places where the personal, the political, and pop culture intersect. A recovering slam poet, she twice competed at the National Poetry Slam and has featured at Cornell University, where she studied English Literature, as well as in Los Angeles, Miami, and throughout the San Francisco Bay Area. Lauren sometimes contributes to Black Nerd Problems (blacknerdproblems.com), and her work has appeared in publications such as *PANK*, *Monkeybicycle*, and *The Nervous Breakdown*. She lives in West Oakland with her spouse, kid, and two brown dogs.

She's @fightingwords on Twitter.

COVER MISSIVE

On "These Eyes (The Guess Who)"

by Greta Boesel

"These Eyes (The Guess Who)" is a "cantograph" in which colors and shapes have been assigned to musical notes and creatively arranged to construct a visual representation of the song. This piece is from the artist's "Stakeout" series, comprising songs about watching, about waiting, and about being seen.

Nomadic Press Emergency Fund

Nomadic Press Black Writers Fund

Right before Labor Day 2020 (and in response to the effects of COVID), Nomadic Press launched its Emergency Fund, a forever fund meant to support Nomadic Press-published writers who have no income, are unemployed, don't qualify for unemployment, have no healthcare, or are just generally in need of covering unexpected or impactful expenses.

Funds are first come, first serve, and are available as long as there is money in the account, and there is a dignity centered internal application that interested folks submit. Disbursements are made for any amount up to $300.

All donations made to this fund are kept in a separate account. The Nomadic Press Emergency Fund (NPEF) account and associated processes (like the application) are overseen by Nomadic Press authors and the group meets every month.

On Juneteenth (June 19) 2020, Nomadic Press launched the Nomadic Press Black Writers Fund (NPBWF), a forever fund that will be directly built into the fabric of our organization for as long as Nomadic Press exists and puts additional monies directly into the pockets of our Black writers at the end of each year.

Here is how it works:

$1 of each book sale goes into the fund.

At the end of each year, all Nomadic Press authors have the opportunity to voluntarily donate none, part, or all of their royalties to the fund.

Anyone from our larger communities can donate to the fund. This is where you come in!

At the end of the year, whatever monies are in the fund will be evenly distributed to all Black Nomadic Press authors that have been published by the date of disbursement (mid-to-late December).

The fund (and associated, separate bank account) has an oversight team comprised of four authors (Ayodele Nzinga, Daniel B. Summerhill, Dazié Grego-Sykes, and Odelia Younge) + Nomadic Press Executive Director J. K. Fowler.

Please consider supporting these funds. You can also more generally support Nomadic Press by donating to our general fund via nomadicpress.org/donate and by continuing to buy our books. As always, thank you for your support!

Scan the QR code for more information and/or to donate.

You can also donate at nomadicpress.org/store.